BT
701.2
.S44
063
1988

15⁶⁵

D1239907

ON BEING HUMAN:
Imaging God in the Modern World

Calvin Seerveld

WELCH PUBLISHING COMPANY INC.
Burlington, Ontario, Canada

Settings of the songs are used by permission
of the Christian Reformed Publications,
Grand Rapids, Michigan.

Canadian Cataloguing in Publication Data

Seerveld, Calvin, 1930–
    On being human

ISBN 1–55011–068–3

1. Image of God – Prayer-books and devotions.
2. Man (Christian theology) – Prayer-books and
devotions.   I. Title.

BT701.2.S42 1988   233′.5   C89-093129-1

Welch Publishing Company Inc.
960 The Gateway
Burlington, Ontario
L7L 5K7   Canada

© 1988 Calvin Seerveld

Permission to make the songs and artworks illustrating this book available
to the reading public has been gratefully received from the respective
authorities noted. If any corrections need to be made in awarding credits,
please contact the author.

Cover illustration: **Ernst Barlach,** *Singender Mann* (1928) Bronze, Ernst
Barlach Haus, Hamburg

Printed in Canada
Cover and book design, typography: Willem Hart

CONTENTS

for Inès, Oma and Dad
for Anya and Tim,
Gioia and Jim, Luke and Jan

Rembrandt van Rijn, *Zelfportret Tekenend* (1648)
Etching, Rosenwald Collection National Gallery of Art,
Washington, D.C.

When Rembrandt portrays himself he always catches the
ambiguous seriousness of being human. La gloire et le
misère de l'homme is presented. His humans have double
chins and girth; they would never win North American
beauty contests. Rembrandt is seen busy drawing in a sketch
book, before a sunlit window, half-hidden in the shadows
that give the calling of his lifework depth.

INTRODUCTION

How can we know what it means to be "human"? Or do we take for granted that we are acting humanly simply because we were born a man or a woman?

A humanist, like Pico della Mirandola (*On the dignity of being human*, 1496), has always believed in the godliness of human nature: if we men and women try hard enough, we can become like God, and we shall make this earth our paradise. But wars and starving children, criminality, depression and adult fear remain at large in the human race, giving the lie to the humanist creed and its false gospel of control and domination.

To get it straight — what being human is, according to God — one should listen to Scripture. What does the Bible say makes us human? Why are human creatures special in the world? What do we do about our inhumanity?

Psalm 8 catches the matter of being human neatly. We two-legged sons and daughters of Adam and Eve look puny under a heaven of stars, yet we were made almost like God! Humans were given the special task of leading everything under the sun into praise of the Lord. We humans, however, are such ungainly creatures. Rembrandt gets it right in his engravings. Rembrandt never idolizes the human creature, but presents human glory with the weaknesses showing.

These translations of Scripture passages and meditations were originally presented at a conference in Zeist, the Netherlands, for professors and students and also non-academic people who were interested in Christian philosophy. This international conference of learned lectures and workshops was sponsored by the Association for Calvinist Philosophy. Because a Christian philosophy naturally breathes with the pulse of the Bible, the organizers of the conference wanted also to hear the Scriptures speak directly to the selected topic, "On being human."

My friend Robert Vander Vennen has helped me edit the original pieces for a broader audience. My friend Willem Hart has given the text the aesthetically enhancing, visual context I so deeply desired. A person is blessed who has good friends.

I come from the Reformed Christian tradition which has normally understood our human imaging of God to be found in assuming the vice-regent Rule of creation. Participating in the kingdom Rule of Christ is the obedient service expected of humans who are working out their salvation freely given them by Jesus Christ. I continue to believe this is biblically sound.

These meditations also highlight a few scriptural truths that may update the Reformed heritage and make it sparkle for persons in our day who are weighted down with the cares of the world.

Our deeply embedded human *fragility* is not an offence to the Lord but is God's choice for co-workers (see I Corinthians 1:26-31, Ephesians 2:8-10). *Melchizedek* is the watchword which may protect us men and women from letting pride worm itself into the solid faith community of the Reformation so prone to worldwide, Christian action. *Pregnant* can make us aware that our being human is to be characterized by an ongoing labour and expectancy.

Such is the direction Scripture gives for us to understand our being human.

The songs included are for singing. The artworks represented are for imaginative viewing. The Scripture translations and prayers are meant to be read aloud and heard.

Humans should also use a book humanly. That means, one is called to enjoy it in the living presence of God, as a listening sinner or as sinful saint, sharing its truth with one's neighbour.

Calvin Seerveld
Sabbatical year, January 1987

PSALM 8

1 LORD God how great your won-der-ful cre-a - tion!
2 A - mazed at night I scan the sky and lin - ger
3 LORD, you have made us hu -mans tru - ly lord - ly,
4 LORD God how great your won-der-ful cre-a - tion!

Your Name re - sounds through earth each gen - er - a - tion.
to see the moon and stars made by your fin - ger
crowned us with cul - ti - vat - ing might and glo - ry.
Your Name is heard at large by ev - ery na - tion.

Weak ba - by cries still cel - e - brate your laws.
What good are mor - tal hu - mans on the earth?
Mar - vel - lous crea - tures— bird and fish and beast—
Grant us the grace and wise hu - mil - i - ty

Your stun - ning deeds make e - ven scof - fers pause.
Why do you gent - ly care for us from birth?
You have sub - ject - ed un - der -neath our feet.
to claim and serve your rul - ing ma - jes - ty.

Text: Psalm 8; vers. Calvin Seerveld, 1986, ©
Tune: Louis Bourgeois, 1551, harm. Chris Thomas, 1983

11 11 10 10 Genevan 8

1. MEANT TO PRAY

Ernst Barlach, *Schwebender Gottvater* (1922) Bronze, Ernst Barlach Haus, Hamburg

John Calvin's favourite picture of God the Father was found in Exodus 34:6-7. "The LORD, the LORD God, a God merciful and gracious, slow to anger, and abounding in covenanting, faithful love...." Barlach presents God compassionately reaching out and blessing the creatures God loves, tends, and judges, waiting intently to hear our praise and prayer.

MEANT TO PRAY

First we shall read Psalm 139 and then a paragraph from the letter God had Paul write down for the church at Philippi. This is the Word of God:

You have dug into my life, LORD, and know me utterly.
My sitting down and my standing up—you know that!
My provisional thought(s) you are sensitive to from far away.
My just walking around and my lying down you surround
with your presence.
Every one of my quirks (I see) you are intimately familiar
with.
There is not a word on my tongue that you, LORD God, do not
know exactly.
Behind me and ahead of me, you have held me tight.
You touched me with your hand—
    It's all too extraordinary, it's just beyond me!
    I can't understand such attention!

Is there anywhere I could wander where your spirit would
not be?
Is there any place I could run away from your being nearby?
If I climbed up into the heavens, you would be there.
If I had to sleep in the grave, there, (LORD) you are too!
Were I to take the wings of the red early morning sky
and let myself drift way down to the most remote spot of the
sea,
even there your hand could touch me,
your right arm would hold me tight.
Talking to myself, I said,
but the Dark, an unhappy gloom, might cover me from sight;

the Night, I'm afraid, will swallow me up—!
But Darkness is not darkness with you,
and Night is as shining as day,
because you created my very insides!
You delicately braided me together inside the womb of my
mother—
thank you, (LORD!) that I am so amazingly specially treated!
Whatever you do is most extraordinarily marvellous!

You know my self to the core.
Even though I was conceived in a secluded chamber and
artfully composed, as it were, in the lowest bowels,
my finest bones are not invisible to you.
Your eyes saw me when an unformed child!
Each one of my days being fashioned—not one of them
missing!—
stand written in your book—
O God! How unfathomable to me are your doings!
How overpowering are all of them together!
Were I to count them up, they would number more than the
grains of sand on the shore.
—when I am waked (from death), I will still be with you!

O God, would you kill those faithless, godless ones?!
Get away from me you unholy, bloody men!
Those who rebel against you with a smile,
who use your name for the show?
Those who hatefully neglect you, LORD God, shouldn't I hate
them?
those who stand up against you?—can I help it if they make
me stomach-sick?
      I hate them with a pure hatred.
      They are enemies to me, too.

O God! Dig into my life and know me heart to heart.
Test, probe, purify me! and pierce through my thoughts.
See whether I be on a road headed for grief,
and take me by the hand (instead) on the way of eternal life.

Psalm 139

I entreat Euodia and I entreat Syntyche to get the same habit of thought in the LORD. Yes, I even ask you, my bona fide colleague, to assist these women who laboured side by side with me in bringing the good news, together with Clement and the rest of my fellow workers whose names are in the Book of Life.

Rejoice in the LORD at all times! I'll say it again: keep on rejoicing! Let your forbearance be known to all kinds of people—the LORD is nearby! Do not be overanxious about anything, but in every kind of thing let your requests be known firsthand to God in prayer, in pleading, couched in thanksgiving. Then the shalom of God which surpasses all understanding will surely protect your hearts and your intentions in Christ Jesus.

Philippians 4:2-7

A good way to begin to know our humanness is to hear the God of Psalm 139 speak. This Scripture tells us that to be a human creature is to be coram Deo, to live before the face of God, not just as a fact you could learn, but as a lived experience. God knows you to the core of your human selfhood. We humans are creatures God knows heart to heart. Because we humans without exception worship, each one of us is consciously or self-unconsciously aware of the fact that the LORD's faithful, all-encompassing care attends us and penetrates past the maintenance of each hair of our head and touches us in our self-identity because God has wonderfully formed us in our mother's womb. Psalm 139 reveals the truth that the peculiar feature of human creatures is that the Creator LORD holds us to be accountable persons in God's holy presence.

Animals, plants and rocks exist coram Deo, too, and respond gloriously to God's will in their own way as animals, plants and rocks. Lions stalking prey deep in the jungle are looking to God for their food, says Scripture (Psalm 104:14-30). The colours with which God clothes wildflowers are a praise more exquisite than Solomon's finery, says Scripture (Matthew 6:25-34). The reaches of sky which give play-room to clouds jubilantly proclaim the stunning majesty of the LORD, says Scripture (Psalm 19:1-4). The bird, tree and stone on every street-corner witness that the God of the Scriptures revealed in Jesus

Christ is LORD of heaven and earth, even before humans built their cities (see Job 38-41)!

Non-human creatures often respond to God more surely than we humans do.   Deborah ends her stirring song by pleading that God's children may become servants as faithful as the sun which every day rises and runs like a brilliant bridegroom through the sky (Judges 5:31, Psalm 19:4c-6). Psalm 8 is not a humanist manifesto, encouraging us lordly ones to dominate non-human creatures. To follow the evil path of domination is to reap the environmental whirlwind we now face. Psalm 8 puts humans in their place. We are insignificant next to the stars and moon in the night sky.

But the sun and the stars—God knows each one by name (Psalm 147:4)—and the moon, which changes the tides of water bodies on the earth and winks young men and women into enfolding their arms, and the deep-growing Kentucky blue-grass and butterflies sprung from cocoons—all these do not pray. The glossolalia of non-human creatures fills the universe and testifies to the true God's glory, but the animal cry for sustenance is mute, diseased trees suffer wordlessly, waiting for the redemption of our human bodies (Romans 8:19-25), and when the LORD angrily shakes mountains to their foundations, the rock makes no protest (Psalm 104:31-32; see Habakkuk 3). Only human creatures can pray and fight back with God. The response of animals, plants and rocks is more like the selfless service of the mighty angels today. To be in God's presence, in-escapably responsible yourself for being obedient or disobedi-ent to the LORD—that fulcrum of being existentially directed toward God or else with your back to the LORD is at the bottom of what is special about being a human creature. Only the human creature lives out of a committed (or wrongly directed) faith.

It may seem to you that the scriptural point "human life is religion in action" is a commonplace. There can be no argument that lifting up our hearts in joyful worship—sursum corda—cannot make sense even to the most intelligent, problem-solving, species-sensitive apes. We may debate how best to think through and formulate in our philosophical anthropol-ogy the distinctive heart-directionality of human nature—the

fact that a man or a woman is at core a committed servant of the
LORD as created or else stands in fundamental rebellion against
God, which moulds everything else that person does. We may
debate how best to avoid conflating our structural knowledge
of the heart-direction of human nature with our subjective
human activity of believing, that functional dimension of con-
fessional certainty which always reflects whatever a man or
woman's basic allegiance happens to be. But it is alone the
troubled glory of humanity, Scripture leads us to say, to be a
creature able to pray, whose very existence is the properly
awestruck expectation of being led by the Word and Spirit of
the LORD.

Again, if this sounds familiar and overly complete as
orientation, we still have not heard Psalm 139 and Philippians
4 speak. This is not a series of Bible-study "lessons" or a
devotional exercise to round off the day as a custom before
sleep. The Scriptures, when read, are a call to everyone within
hearing to meet the LORD revealed in Jesus Christ by the power
of his Word, to be humbled and made sad or to be surprised by
joy at the miracle of our humanity, able to hear and see God's
voice and face.

Psalm 139 exemplifies, proclaims and asks us to bask in the
incredible attention and fulfilling security that God provides
for us humans, especially for believers (see 1 Timothy 4:1-10).
Your quirks and kinks, from the time your umbilical cord was
severed until your remains settle back into the dust of the grave
(if such be your lot before Christ returns) are lovingly known,
compassionately judged and up for redemption by the LORD.
Since you are human, you are either awfully glad that nothing
can separate you from the Psalm 139 love of God revealed in
Jesus Christ, or you have missed the good news of our Scripture.

We misread Psalm 139, I believe, if we take it to be the
revelation of a threatening, omniscient divinity whose Equus
Eye haunts sinners with punishment for the slightest infrac-
tion. No, the psalmist has the strength and maturity of faith to
feel covered by the Lord's all-pervasive grace and then even to
ask for God to finish off the perpetrators of institutionalized
evil. That curse (verses 19-22) is not a vindictive Old Testament

throwback but the anguished request of a persecuted believer, available to New Testament followers of the Christ, too, that God end the corporate lie, the bureaucratic power trip, the nauseous media hype. The imprecation of Psalm 139 applies wherever human sin is given anonymity, also toward the apostate church, Babylon, according to the New Testament (see Revelation 17-18). But immediately after the curse has escaped his lips, the psalmist catches his breath and takes an oath: "O God! Search me through and through; test and refine me lest my heart be impure and I not know what your holy will is" (verses 23-24). Only the pure-in-heart humans, the men and women who do what is right, may issue injunctions on evil and plead for God's redemptive acts (see Psalm 137:4-6, which precedes 137:7-9; see also James 5:13-20).

That's why Paul's imperative of Philippians 4 follows up Psalm 139's indicative about the Lord's amazing providence so well with its concrete directives: you people covered by Christ's blood are called by the LORD to develop the same habit of mind, to become one by heart-and-deed living. My colleagues, says Paul, in the joy of the Lord's abiding faithfulness and caring presence, do not be overly anxious about everything under the sun, trying to set it straight yourself as if you can say, "Here's the kingdom!"; "No, there it is!" (see Luke 17:20-24). Learn instead how to become together a constant prayer=offering=living sacrifice (Romans 12:1-2), a healing fellowship of humans that enjoys and dispenses the shalom of the LORD. To keep on rejoicing does not mean that you keep an airline-stewardess smile pasted on your face. To be ever joyful in the LORD means that you experience your humanity as a fruit-bearing gift of God.

We humans are either at home with the God of Psalm 139 and the imperative to let hurts and anger and uptightness go, or we are displaced persons in God's world, human dropouts who will find many devices to pacify the deep-rooted, weary uneasiness of remaining closed off before the Creator and Redeemer. At home with the LORD we dissolve into the simple joy the body of Christ knows, where we as stand-up humans plead on our knees before the Holy One to make us pure in heart and intention and in actual deed toward our brother and sister in Christ, winsome toward our neighbour.

For humans who know the truth and respond by not doing it, it is sin (James 4:17). For those of us humans who hear the LORD speak and deeply want to obey, we may sing Psalm 139 to the LORD with heart and voice.

O LORD,
thank you for the gift of our humanity,
that we are not sticks or stones, vegetation or animals,
but creatures—less impressive than the stars, but wonderfully
        fashioned—
able to speak to you, our LORD,
to pray in response to your Word, your deed.
So we beseech you, LORD, and entreat one another,
to ready us for your Spirit's moulding us into the mind of Christ,
that we may truly become Christ's body in a communal
        consciousness,
joyful about our tasks in the world.
Teach us to wonder in awe at the humanity you have given us.
Help us to be human as we walk the everlasting way
in the name of Jesus Christ.
    Amen.

PSALM 139

1 LORD, you have searched my life and know each move I make, each
2 Where can I hide, where can I flee? There is no place you
3 You formed me in my moth-er's womb, you braid-ed me with
4 O LORD, de - stroy the vi - o - lent who speak of you with

step I go; my half - framed talk, my in - most thought— you
do not see. No dis - tant grave, no for - eign place can
awe - some care; my flesh, my un - formed bones grew there in -
ill in - tent. I shrink from those who hate your name, from

watch and note my to - tal walk. Your hand keeps hold of
bar me from your strong em - brace. I can - not be ob -
vis - i - ble, yet seen by you. Your won - ders make me
en - e - mies who feel no shame. LORD, search my heart, teach

me al - ways; your knowl - edge leaves me mute, a - mazed.
scured by night: your Spir - it pierc - es dark with light.
catch my breath, sur - round - ing me in life, in death.
me, I pray, to walk the ev - er - last - ing way.

Text: Psalm 139; vers. Calvin Seerveld, 1985, ©
Tune: John Bishop, 1711, harm. Harry E. Wooldridge, 1845-1917

88 88 88 LEICESTER

2. PRONE TO SIN

Rembrandt van Rijn, *Adam en Eva* (1638) Etching, Rosenwald Collection, National Gallery of Art, Washington, D.C.

Rembrandt does not idealize the Adam and Eve before the fall. Their fleshly bodies and uncertain gestures bespeak a roughhewn vigour and human ability to wrestle with decisions, even in paradise. The happy elephant in the background and the formidable reptile in the tree above them give world dimensions to what is at stake in their human temptation to act like God.

W̶e read first Leviticus 19, a couple of paragraphs of what Luther called "an exposition of the Ten Words," given on Mount Sinai. This is the Word of God:

> And the LORD said to Moses: Tell the whole congregation of Israelite children, tell them, "You are all to be holy, because I the LORD your God am holy."
>
> "Let each of you respect your mother and your father. Everyone is to take good care of my sabbaths—I am the LORD your God.
>
> "Do not turn away toward no-gods; don't put together homemade gods for yourselves—I am the LORD your God!
>
> "...Do not do what is crooked in matters of rights and just claims. You are never to be partial toward the poor, and you must never defer to the great; but you are to judge your neighbour with a just-dealing integrity. You may not walk around among your people slandering: never take a stand against the very life-blood of your neighbour—I am the LORD."
>
> "You shall not hate your brother or sister in your heart, but you are openly to set things straight with your neighbour so that you do not become guilty because of his or her sin; but you are not to take vengeance, you are not to bear a grudge against any one of your people: you are to love your neighbour as yourself—I am the LORD."

Leviticus 19:1-4, 15-18

Now read a parable of Jesus that God had recorded by the tax collector Matthew, who had become an apostle of the Lord. The

setting of the parable in the last chapters of Matthew's account
is important. The Jewish nation had just repudiated historically the Messiah's Rule, and its candlestick as a people was
now to be removed—that's why Jesus wept on that triumphant,
lowly ass (see Luke 19:28-44). After this historic rejection by the
house of Israel, Jesus housecleaned the commercialized temple
to the hosannas of the handicapped whom he healed (Matthew
21:12-17); Jesus publicly cursed a fig tree that had leaves on it
but no fruit (21:18-22). Then the leaders of God's people said,
"By whose authority do you commit civil disobedience and
cause a stir in the temple?" Jesus asked, "Was the baptism of
John a prophetic, heavenly act or an ego trip?" The leaders said
they didn't know. Then, in the catechetical wiseman style the
rabbis practised, Jesus pointedly continued:

What do you people think about this?
A man had two children. Approaching the first one, the
father said, "My child, go work today in the vineyard." And
the first one answered, "I will not go." But later on the first
one changed his mind and went to work.
Approaching the second one, the father said the same
thing. And the second child answered, "Yes, sir." But the
second one did not go.
Which of the two did the will of the father?
The chief priests and the elders of the people said,
"The first one."
So Jesus said to them, "Let me tell you something. The
tax collectors and the prostitutes are ahead of you in the
kingdom Rule of God. (The Baptizer) John came to you, you
know, in the Way of doing-what-is-right, and you didn't trust
him; but the tax collectors and prostitutes took him at his
word. Even when you people saw (what happened among
sinners who repented and believed), you didn't change your
mind afterwards so that you could have believed John's
message."
...Jesus said to them: "Haven't you even read aloud in
Psalm 118:22-23
'The very stone which the builders rejected after testing has
become the uniting keystone—

this is indeed the LORD's doing,
and it is marvellous in our eyes!'?
Therefore, I tell you that the kingdom Rule of God will
be taken away from you (leaders), and will be given to a
people who produce the fruits of God's rule."

Matthew 21:28-32, 42-43

By calling us all to be holy, Scripture reveals that as a matter of
historical fact we human creatures are not holy. Indeed, since
Adam and Eve disobeyed God in the beginning, it is a mark of
humanity to be sinful, prone to sin (Romans 5:12-17). Thanks
to our being specially structured, selfhooded, responsible creatures before the LORD, it is we humans who give character to sin.
Sin is living godlessly out of and for your self. It is a humanist
mistake to describe something sinful as "bestial," as if men
were centaur and women were mermaid combinations of an-
gelic intelligence with animalic flesh and sometimes the beast
gets the better of the beauty.

No, animals do not sin, no more than animals can pray.
The enormity of Nazi crime is that it was human. And though
devils apparently can be relentlessly perverse, evil powers, I
dare say that torture and hypocrisy, the epitome of sin, if you
will, the most hardened sort, show how human sin is—you
break down your neighbour's self, or you pretend that you
yourself are not responsible for any ill. Sin is a fundamental
human negation of our awestruck nature: sin is essentially
proud, heartless selfishness.

I'm not interested right now in trying to develop a few
dogmatic theses which might circumscribe what can be biblically confessed about sin. Nor do I want to move from there
analytically to how a Christian (that is, scripturally led) philosophical anthropology should take account of sin in its discussion of human act-structure, relative norms and societal re-
form. Instead, let us hear simply what the Gospel of Matthew
and the book of Leviticus say about our sin, since the Bible is not
a treatise "out there" but is the LORD speaking to us right here.

Matthew the tax collector knew where the believing estab-
lishment put him and his profession: with the prostitutes,

organized sin and premeditated corruption. Imagine his joyful pain upon recording Christ's severe teaching to the chief priests and ruling elders of God's people that ahead of them in line for administering Messiah's Rule were the prostitutes and tax collectors, Jewish Roman army sergeants and ignorant rabble who had repented under the preaching of Baptizer John and followed John's instructions on doing what the law had always required: Love your neighbour as yourself, fulfil your neighbour's need by sharing your goods, exercise your office within the ordained limits of its service, show you are a forgiven person by being merciful (Luke 3:1-14, Matthew 18:21-35).

It would be upsetting for a Jew like Matthew to realize that the emphasis put by the leaders of his people on keeping the law had been futile because it was not rooted in a truly humbled awareness of one's helplessness in sin. But Matthew threw a feast for his fellow sinners when he gave up everything to follow Jesus and came to understand that to obey the LORD in willing deed is all that counts, not following the right prescriptions to the letter and drawing out the correct implications (Matthew 9:9-13, Luke 5:27-39).

This good news of Matthew and the simple direction of Leviticus may seem to run counter to everything we educated Christian believers would expect, too, we who want to chew the meat of a sanctified life in society and history rather than just keep on drinking the milk of salvation.

Scripture is clear that Jesus Christ's message and deeds surpassed Baptizer John's powerful ministry of introducing God's Rule on earth (Luke 7:24-30, Acts 18:24-28). Christ's birth, death, resurrection and ascension ended the old period of temporizing sacrifices designed to keep judgement at bay from our sins until God finally would act for us, because Christ's sacrifice was God in action once and for all, making good completely for the sin of us humans who were lost (see Hebrews 8-10).

But Scripture is also clear that Christ's liberating kingdom Rule is founded in the Baptizer John's call for us sinners to lead a repentant holy life of right-doing. Leviticus is not abrogated by the Newer Testament (Matthew 5:17-20, 43-48). The call to holiness is not a call to ritual purification, to separation from contact with what is evil, for us to leave this "world" of human cultivation behind. Instead, the call to be holy, the call to sainthood, is the invitation to give up our self-righteousness, to become identified singly by Christ's forgiveness for us in our particular, rebellious, unlovely idiosyncrasy, and for us to flourish in that new certified identity. Holiness, according to the Bible, is not a state of purity humans can struggle to achieve. Holiness is a gracious gift of God which those humans exercise who, in dismay at their cheeky self-certainty, give in to the proffered adoption by Christ and then simply and meekly live out the fruits of the Holy Spirit within them.

Is it wrong to say that most of us probably tend to fit the pattern of the second child in Jesus' parable recorded in Matthew 21? You might say that we appear less like prodigal sons and daughters and more like the respectable eldest, hard-working son who didn't join the dance of celebration when the sinning brother was restored to his father (Luke 15:11-32). We do not ignore God's will to respect our parents, protect God's day of celebrative rest and avoid the fabrication of idols. We also know better than to suppress the truth of the new covenant in Christ's blood typified by forgiveness, which makes work-righteousness a farce of unrighteousness. We know that we have to lose the life we covet in order to receive our own life back for keeps in Christ's body. But with all our knowledge—as great a learning as that of the scribes and Pharisees, even more—with our good philosophical theorizing, are we maturing in an understanding and life of holiness? Or do we still try to hide in a fortress of scholastic verities?

Scripture asks us humans whose hypocritically hardening ears can still hear to abandon our pet peeves and partialities, to end our permissivenesses, our grudges and our residual self-satisfaction, and to begin to bear fruit—theoretical fruit, too, if we are theoreticians—worthy of repentance. That means that those of us who are philosophers need to foster and build a philosophical anthropology that heals fractured theories of humanity and gives a younger generation of scholars not just a head full of split-hair concepts but horizons within which to think integratively. We are faithful to God's Word in our philosophizing not merely when our analysis is logically correct and paired with right living but when our thinking is truly thanking, when our theory sparkles with life-giving wisdom. Good Christian philosophy is only a "yes, sir" exercise, mere leaves on the fig tree, mere verbiage, not a real fruit-bearing offering unless its thoughtful, systematic contribution to a right ordering of life is permeated by the contagious spirit of love, joy, peace, mercy and gentle thankfulness which is of a piece with life hidden in the Christ, where bearing one another's burdens—conceptual burdens, too—is indeed fulfilling the law of Leviticus and of Christ (see Galatians 5:22-6:2).

Dear LORD,
We pray that your Spirit will make the reading of these meditations fruitful,
that you will show us how to be holy in our thinking, speaking, feeling,
reaching out to one another.
Please save us from being crooked, from wrong-doing,
from rejecting the blessing you have provided in Jesus Christ
which can break down all our barriers, deceit and human sinfulness.
Hear us as we pray and sing and listen to the simple, comforting direction of your Word.
We ask for much grace today, in the name of Jesus Christ.
Amen.

LEVITICUS 19

1 Be just in judg-ment, fair to all, be-have re-spon-si-bly.
2 Do not dis-tort your neigh-bor's deed or har-bor se-cret hate.
3 No ven-geance is with-in your right; you may not bear a grudge.

De-fer to nei-ther poor nor great: act with in-teg-ri-ty.
Deal o-pen-ly with those at fault so your own life is straight.
But love your neigh-bor as your-self; hear me, the right-eous Judge.

1-2
I am the LORD.

Final ending
I am the LORD!

Text: Leviticus 19:15-18; vers. Calvin Seerveld, 1985
Tune: Calvin Seerveld, 1985; harm. Dale Grotenhuis, 1986
Text and music © 1987, Calvin Seerveld

86 86 4 TORONTO

3.FRAGILE

Ernst Barlach, *Das Wiedersehen* (1926) Walnut wood, Ernst
Barlach Haus, Hamburg

Barlach chisels a tender stillness into the figure of Christ
bending the head to accept Thomas' surrender of belief. We
people are bodily so frail, not only in physique but also in
keeping promises and in holding certainties. A reunion too,
after time has elapsed, often finds the happiness blurred by
the curve of recognition that opportunities between us have
been missed, and are gone. Humans have a once-only kind
of fragility.

FRAGILE

Psalm 139 and Philippians 4 reveal the special calling of humans to live before God entirely as an act of prayer. Leviticus 19 and Matthew 21 reveal our historical inability and unwillingness to be holy — as a matter of fact, we are sinful. Now hear Scripture that shows another dimension of being human: being fragile.

First we read Psalm 39. This is the Word of God.

Once upon a time I said to myself: I have got to watch out for my attitude or there will be sinning with my tongue. I have got to muzzle my mouth as long as the wicked are nearby me — or there will be sinning with my tongue.

So I stopped my tongue from even moving. I kept still. But rather than get better, my vexation grew more agitated. I got all hot inside; I started getting burned up; I had to set my tongue loose and talk.

So I said: Lord God! Lord God...tell me...about the outcome, the end of the affair of me; and tell me how many days I still have so that I may realize what a perishable thing I am. Yes, you made my days about as broad as a man's hand and my lifetime is like nothing to you — a little hot air, that's all a man makes himself out to be; he walks along like a shadow, getting steamed up about nothing; he tries to get everything stacked up under control and doesn't even know who will take it over after him....

At the same time, Lord! now — what did I want? Oh, yes, I want...my desire! my longing! what I hope for and expect! my request...that goes out to you, Lord, is:

Save me from all my sins.

Do not let me be made the laughingstock of the fools around me!

— I'll keep quiet. I won't open my mouth.

(I know) it is you who afflict me — (But — but, LORD —)
take away the vexing burden under which you weigh me
down, for I have been wasting away under the pressure of
your hand. You discipline a man by punishment for his sins,
and like a clothes-closet moth you eat away his most coveted
prize — yes, a little hot air, that's all a man is....

(But —)

Hear my prayer, LORD. Listen to my cry for help! Do
not be unmoved because I am crying. Remember, I am a
stranger here, a guest, just a sojourning pilgrim like all my
fathers and mothers before me, your guest, LORD.

Don't look at me that way!

Let me become a little more cheerful before I sink away
and am no more....

Psalm 39

Now comes the Holy-Spirited witness of Paul to the Corinthians in 2 Corinthians 5:1-10. This too is the Word of God:

We know that if the earthly housing of our bodily tent be
destroyed, we have a building from God, an everlasting
housing constructed in the heavens without hands.

It's so that in this day and age we longingly groan,
yearning to put on over (what we have) our heavenly habita-
tion, so that by putting it on we will not be found naked.
While we are still in this bodily tent, we complain of being
burdened — not that we want to be unclothed, but rather,
we want to be clothed upon more fully, so that what is
mortal may be swallowed up by life!

God is the one who has made us fit for this very "Operation
Clothing": God has given us the Spirit as earnest money (for the
coming change of clothing).

So we are always confident. We know that while we dwell
in the bodily (tent) we are not inhabiting (the building forthcom-
ing) from the Lord — we walk truly by faith, not by sight. But we
are indeed confident: we might even be ready to leave the bodily
(tent) behind and be at home with the Lord. But that's why,

whether we are dwelling (as bodily tents) or not inhabiting (bodily tents), we are really eager to be well-pleasing to the Lord
  Every one of us is going to appear before the judging seat of the Christ so that each one may receive good or bad, depending on what things he or she has bodily done.

Both these passages are among the richest, if sobering, in Scripture because they show existentially how our earthly human living, fraught with tension, urgency and complaint, can be exercised withal in confidence if we accept in faith that our brief lifetime is a trust from the LORD.

It is important to hear Scripture speak on our utterly God-dependent fragility: we humans live literally on borrowed time. Even more so than fresh raspberries or fresh fish, humans are perishable goods. We pass away, becoming and be-going. We are mortal in a way that animals, plants and rocks which have endings are not mortal. We humans are also mortal in ways unlike angels and devils. Our human, timed existence is a short pilgrimage...to Canterbury, Amsterdam, Toronto or somewhere, of which the eternal LORD keeps a record, say the Scriptures.

This human reality of our once-only, dated walk to the eschaton, when Christ shall complete history plagued by sin, has been variously conceived, avoided and misunderstood by those facing it without the directing light of Scripture.

The Greek Homer (and Aristotle, partly) believed men and women to be mortal because we have blood in our veins rather than ichor (a special ethereal fluid Greek gods supposedly had in their bodies). The fact that our great thinking or heroic exploits may live on forever after we human beings individually expire is, however, the consolation of fame and philosophy, of which even the gods and their tiresome immortality may be jealous.

The Orphic cults of Italy, the Platonic traditions of men and certain Stoic doctrines, on the other hand, denied that humans are essentially perishable. That part of us that counts — the soul, the hegemonic monitor of reason, the conscience or semen divinitatis — is substantially eternal and will survive this vale of tears, they confessed.

It is particularly this anthropological creed of immortality that has compromised and blurred the biblical teaching on the religion, sin and mortality of humans. The Scholastic concept of "contingent being" still credits human creatures with God's almighty attribute, no matter how much countervailing, analogical skulduggery one presses into lower-case service. I like the title "On being human" better than "On human being" because it keeps our human existence adjectival, gerundive, rather than a substantial and nominative. I think it can be seen that the preening piety of the philosophical phrase "contingent being" has lasted as a dominant assumption supporting the whole secularization of philosophical theory because philosophy has remained largely "academic" and has hardly ever questioned whether our theoretical reflection will last and is worthwhile and is not deeply relativized by our resident mortality.

The show of humility in the professional pragmatist's pose of waiting for the outcome of one's reflection — did it work? — before one modestly claims relative permanence for one's ideas, still banks on the durability of human power. And the existentialistic belief that our human being-there is really a being-towards-death is also not a biblical recognition of our historical sinfulness as humans. Instead, the existentialists misread the curse upon human sin as a crack in God's world that is structurally given with creatureliness.

To all such aberrant interpretations of human mortality and supposed immortality Psalm 39 and 2 Corinthians 5 present a sharply different, radical perspective found throughout Scripture. They show that only Jesus Christ has immortality (1 Timothy 6:13-16), that humans remain intact only by the grace of a life-breath given them temporarily by God (Genesis 2:7, Ecclesiastes 12:7). They show that how we spend our breathing life span and earthly sojourn has everlasting consequences. Scripture gives us the awesome revelation that once God takes back our life-breath (or transforms our "flesh and blood" at Christ's return — see 1 Corinthians 15:50), then we either "put on immortality" because we have passed from death to life during our pilgrimage (John 5:24) and are covered by Christ's having triumphed over death once and for all (1 Corinthians

15:51-56), or without breath we remain dead in our sin and are raised up only for the judgement to go to hell for keeps, zu Grunde gehen (John 5:28-29, Galatians 6:7-8).

Second Corinthians 5 assumes that humans become God's sheep or else settle down as goats (see Matthew 25:31-46) and spells out clearly that the sheep, those who follow the Christ in deed and have received the Holy Spirit, are signed and sealed to be delivered from the burdened mortality which is our human condition in this day and age. Do not be afraid of the unknown, writes Paul to faithful believers; in fact, later on will prove to be better for us than now! Now we walk around in our underwear, so to speak, tenting, exposed to harm. When the LORD completes his good work on us who form his body, then we will receive a princely set of clothes, a genuinely constructed lordly house, rather than our tents — as different as a stalk of ripened grain is from the seed one drops in the ground — but to each it will be his or her own glorious suit of clothes (1 Corinthians 15:35-44). Therefore do not lose heart, writes Paul, because of sickness, emotional breakdowns, mental distur-bance — any historical trouble. Be of good cheer and confi-dence in the restoration coming because that shalom will outlast forever what keeps us off balance now (2 Corinthians 4:16-18).

What is so powerful about Psalm 39 is that it exercises Paul's New Testament confidence and certainty with gutsy Older Testament candour. The earlier covenanted folk of God, before Christ was born of a woman and the Holy Spirit was poured out on all kinds of people, saw their salvation only in mirrored script (Hebrews 11:13-16, 39-40; see 1 Corinthians 13:12). But believers, like the psalmists, had a tenacious hold of God by faith and never hid their lived pain. Whether it was a wasting illness, the loud prosperity of unbelievers next door or the unkind cuts of friends that was driving the writer of Psalm 39 mad does not matter. It is the passionate trust in which the fellow hollers at God because of the thorn in the flesh that is instructive for us.

"I know I am only a little hot air, LORD, but I know my Leviticus 25:23, where you say we are sojourning guests in your land, landed immigrants in the promised land, pilgrims in your rich creation, holding it in trust. But then treat us more like visitors, LORD! Be more hospitable! Why like a moth do you eat away with cancer the life of my friend? Why do you let soldiers brutally rape women in the defenceless countryside as if you looked the other way? Why do you let fools run so many things! — I'll keep quiet. I know, it is my sin you need to forgive. But — we are your guests, LORD!"

All flesh is grass (Isaiah 40:6-8). All human flesh is grass that suffers bodily in ways the trees and animals and mountainsides cannot know because we humans in our underwear fragility are held personally accountable by the LORD for walking on the Way of life while we are still fragile! The fact that our weakness is troubled by our sin and other evil afoot in the world, compounded by the death that is punishment for sin, complicates sorting things out. But our Scripture reveals that God is the Creator of our human fragility and takes our temporality seriously and approves of our screaming in faith at God when the hurt simply gets to be too much and we really need him to come quickly to give us who hang on by the skin of our faith the new change of clean clothes.

Who of us has the maturity of faith to call the almighty LORD of heaven and earth a moth in our prayers — who has the temerity of faith to cry out, when our loved one is attacked by an incurable cancerous disease, and associate the living God with a moth? Can we recite Psalm 91 believingly when the evil comes so close? Maybe that is the kind of righteous prayer which changes things in God's world (see James 5:13-18).

Who of us has the Holy Spirited wisdom to forge anthropological concepts that sweat tears or to think through ideas that will bleed with dismay at the inhumanity of man to men and women today? Does our philosophical theory tend to be intellectualistically antiseptic because we are sheltered, salaried, relatively free from the fear of molestation?

Each of us in the mainstream of the Western world is a rich person, according to the Bible. We know how hard it is to be humbly generous when we are rich. How difficult it is, says Scripture, to be selflessly busy in the persecuted anticipation of Christ's Rule on earth (Matthew 19:16-30). But if the Scripture before us can break through our defences, it can direct us rich young thinkers and shopkeepers, professionals and rulers to let the promise of 2 Corinthians 5 and the open pain of faith expressed in Psalm 39 begin to permeate our professional activity, our business dealings, our teaching and our holding authority over others.

With all our getting of knowledge on the basic needs and rights, potential, responsibilities and benefits due human nature, we need to recognize the reality of variability and change also built into being human (which has its own law requiring obedience). And with all our comprehension of the creatural changes proper to being human, we need to find redemptive room in our understanding for the special fragility of our humanity. Then our grasp of being human will breathe true suffering confidence and show the troubled cheer that Scripture says comes with our birthright of being human.

Dear LORD of the wonderful creation
and the precariousness of our human lives so dear to you,
we ask that you please give us the mind of Christ
so that we may learn to obey you, wrestle with you,
follow through on what your Word commands
until we count on blessing,
if not always now, then surely soon,
in the next generation of faithful ones,
or when you come in glory with the clothing that will end all tears
and mistakes and deadends.

Although whatever our daily work may be is only a piece of
your service, LORD,
we pray that you make it a coat of many colours
so that it create joy and hope among the younger believing ones
even if it provoke jealousy or spite from those who disbelieve your
Rule.

Thank you for the happy task to be redemptive in our normal
activity,
and we are confident that you will establish the work of our believ-
ing hands and hearts and minds.

Please handle us with care, dear Jesus, for our sake as well as
yours.
Amen.

PSALM 39

1 Once I said, "I must keep qui - et; else I sin in
2 "LORD, are you re - veal - ing lim - its, how my days look
3 "Why, O Lord, must I be wait - ing when my hope is
4 "But, my LORD, your heav - y bur - den wears me out and
5 "Can you see, LORD, I am cry - ing? Do not spurn my

harsh dis - pute. Just to see the wick - ed near me an - gers
in your sight? Just a breath and fleet - ing shad - ow slip - ping
▸ still in you? Keep me, LORD, from sin and trou - ble, from the
weighs me down. All your dis - ci - pline for sin - ning hurts and
sore un - rest. I pass by like those be - fore me, yet I

me, but I stay mute." Yet I could not hold my fu - ry,
by in use - less flight? Yes, I know our lives are frag - ile,
▸ wrong I would pur - sue. Save me from the fool's loud laugh - ter—
bows me to the ground. Must you eat a - way my trea - sures
claim to be your guest! No more sad - ness— give me glad - ness,

burned to vent my sharp cri - tique; then, at last, I had to speak:
that we seem to work in vain— all we have is oth - ers' gain.
▸ I was si - lent, I for - got: you con - trol my trou - bled lot.
like a moth? I'm but a breath. Are you fac - ing me with death?
be my hope be - fore I cease. LORD, dear LORD, I beg for peace."

Text: Psalm 39; vers. Calvin Seerveld, 1983, ©
Tune: Evan Morgan, 1846-1920

87 87 87 7 TYDDYN LLWYN

Ossip Zadkine, *De verwoeste stad* (1951) Harbour in Rotterdam, Netherlands

Zadkine's towering figure has massive, contorted shapes that tell of an industry building and a city's struggle to be a powerful harbour for the world. But its heart was gutted by Nazi bombers one fine day in May 1940. And the huge arms thrash and plead, as it were, like a Moses appealing to the heavens from which the destruction rained: "Deliver us from evil."

PSALM 91

1 Who - ev - er shel - ters with the LORD and lives with -
2 The faith - ful LORD will spare you death. God's wings will
3 Though thou - sands per - ish at your side, such pun - ish -
4 God gives his an - gels charge of you to guard from
5 "Be - cause you cleave to me in love and know my

in the Al - might - y's shade can say, "My God, in
cov - er you from harm. No ter - ror, sick - ness,
▸ ment shall not touch you. Be - cause the LORD serves
those who per - se - cute. You shall not trip a -
name to call in need, I shall pro - tect and

whom I trust, your ref - uge makes me un - a - fraid!"
night or day, will ev - er cause you grave a - larm.
▸ as your home, God's grace will al - ways see you through.
gainst a stone, but tram - ple ser - pents un - der - foot.
keep you safe with bless - ing, glo - ry, life in - deed."

Text: Psalm 91; vers. Calvin Seerveld, 1985, ©
Tune: Grenoble Antiphoner, 1753

LM DEUS TUORUM MILITUM

4. UP FOR ADOPTION

Flip van der Burgt, *'t Is veel eenvoudiger dan jullie denkt*(1956)
Woodcut, illustration in Bijbel zwart/wit, Amsterdam

To be an adopted child means you are really wanted by the
parents. It turns out God wants us to be like defenceless,
expectant children, ready for Christ's embrace. Van der
Burgt's woodcut depicts the account of Mark 10:13-16, how
Jesus took joy in being crowded by children and the young
in the streets of Judea.

UP FOR ADOPTION

In the letter to the Ephesians Paul says that God picked us up dead out of the dumps of sin and made us alive by the transfusion of Christ's blood (2:1-7). Paul goes on to say:

You have been saved by grace through faith. This being saved by grace through faith is not from you: being saved by grace through faith is the gift of God — it is not a matter of (our) works, lest anyone should boast. We are really God's handiwork, and were created in Christ Jesus on the basis of Christ's good works. God prepared Christ's good works beforehand (before we were there) so that we could walk around in their strength (rather than in our own deadly offenses and sins, verse 2).

Ephesians 2:8-10

I continue the point with Paul's discussion in Romans 8 that those who are indwelt by the Holy Spirit are indeed to live as Spirit-filled people.

Do you get the point, then, brothers and sisters? We sinners are not meant to live according to sin because we are sinful, for if you live according to the rule of sin, you are headed for death. But if indwelt by the Spirit you put to death the (evil) deeds of your bodily existence, then you will stay alive.
    Right? All those who are led by the Spirit of God — they are children of God. Now, you did not receive a spirit of bondage, (to throw you) back again into fear (of not being able to save yourself by keeping the law): you received the spirit of adoption (by God). In that spirit of being God's

adopted children we bawl out "Abba!" Our Father —   It is
that very Spirit which reinforces and reverberates along with
our spirit as it testifies that we are children of God!

If we are God's children, why — then we are God's
heirs! If we are God's heirs, we are co-heirs with Christ — at
least if we suffer along with him in order that we may also be
glorified with him. And it is my judgement that the sufferings
of the time right now are not even worth comparing with the
coming glory that will be revealed to us.

There is an eager longing of creation waiting steadily for
this final, unveiling revelation of glory of the sons and daughters of God. Creation was not voluntarily subjected to mean-
inglessness but fell through Adam and Eve's subjecting it,
albeit with hope, because this same creation will be liberated
from the bondage of decay and be given the glorious freedom
of God's children.

We know that the whole creation is groaning together
and suffering labour pains right up till now. Not only creation but we ourselves, too, who have a headstart (on glory)
with the presence of the Holy Spirit, even we groan along in
ourselves, intently anticipating the full adoption (by God), the
actual redemption of our present corporeality....

Romans 8:12-23

Romans 8 goes on, as you know, to close with a paean of
certainty on what it means to be a Spirit-filled, adopted child of
God. But instead of that, I'm going to conclude our reading of
Scripture with that existential, apocalyptic hymn for God's
children from the Older Testament, Psalm 149.

O hallelu Yahweh!

Sing to the LORD God a new song!
Sing God's praise right there where the ones of faithful piety
come together to discuss things and to celebrate!

Let Israel rejoice in the One who made them.
Let the sons and daughters of Zion jump around joyfully in

exaltation of their king!
Let them praise God's name with dancing!
Let them play stringed instruments for God with tambourines
and guitars.
Yes, the LORD God likes to be happy with God's people —
God will outfit especially those who have been humiliated
   with a resounding triumphant liberation.

Let the faithful folk of piety exult in such shining glory —
Let them even be jubilant on their beds at night —
Let their excited praises of God rise up in their throats...
while they hold a double-edged sword in their hands:
to exercise retribution among the peoples of the world, that
is, corrective punishment on the nations,
to bind their worldly potentates with chains,   constrict their
VIPs with shackles of iron,
to execute on them the just judgement, as it has been written
(Isaiah 45:14, Micah 4:13, Zechariah 10:3-5, 12:6; see also
Revelation 19)
   — this is the glory coming for all those faithful with piety
before God!

O hallelu Yahweh!

Earlier we faced Scripture which highlighted our selfhooded
human nature and encouraged us to be aware that the LORD is
nearby as we humans answer God's call to be obedient servants, doing what is just and caring in the world according to
the Word of truth. Then we read Scripture that pinpointed the
historical sinful status of us humans and disclosed the pulley of
fragility and the promise of glory (Psalm 39 and 2 Corinthians
5) which throw into relief the condition of our good but troubled temporality.
   Now God's Word ups the ante, so to speak, in Ephesians 2,
Romans 8 and Psalm 149 by focusing our attention on the all-
important change that needs to happen in our being human and
our human becoming in God's world: becoming adopted children of God. To be an adopted child of God is no longer simply
given with humanity; it is also not a human achievement. But

becoming an adopted child of God in Jesus Christ's body and being led by the Holy Spirit is a blessing that is critical for saving one's humanity.

We humans were created to be open to the LORD God and at home in God's commanding presence. We know that from Psalm 91. But Adam and Eve's disobedience which implicated all who followed (Romans 5:12-14), left us humans with our backs turned to God, staring at our own shadows, unable to see the created light of day (Matthew 6:22-23, 1 John 1:5-7). So unless humans are historically turned around, grafted into the body of Jesus Christ, given new original roots, as it were, so that men and women may flower as the creatures made specially to image God (Genesis 1:26-31), unless humans become adopted children of God in time and live that way, their humanity goes to seed or rots, says Scripture (Romans 5:15-17, 6:12-23).

To be losing one's humanity does not mean one becomes an animal. Humans who are not born again live in the dark as humans, ignorant of what brings blessing, often cowering before the sun or the moon, animals of prey or fascinating contrivances of their own hands (Acts 17:22-31, Psalm 115, Isaiah 44). Humans who come of age and are faced with the prophetic call to repent of their practical godlessness and to accept God's offer of free salvation and a change to obedient life (Romans 1:16-17) but persist in saying NO grow perverse (Romans 1:18-32). Those losing their humanity become persons of violence, deceit, vanity, malice, witless engorgement (Paul has lists one can refer to, and Paul is writing to communions of saints! See Galatians 5:19-21, 1 Timothy 6:3-5, 2 Timothy 3:1-5).

The fact is that our ongoing humanity is directionally loaded, either becoming lost or becoming saved. Our concrete humanity is never at a standstill. We are either growing in grace, despite lapses in redeemed humanity, or we are growing in sin, with God's gracious restraint upon the corruption of our human nature. The deployment of a given person's intelligence, sensitivity, skill, imaginativity, promise-keeping character and many other gifts is not incidental to our creaturely responsibility as humans, but the development that counts, the key act of one's human becoming, according to Scripture, is whether one's humanity is being filled with the fullness of God

(Ephesians 3:14-19). That development is what the rest of creation is waiting for — the polluted rivers, diseased trees, starving deforested wildlife — not to speak of our neighbours who are hurting, and above all the LORD, who is heartsick at our heedless human revels (see Genesis 6:5-7, James 4:1-10).

I don't want to pursue in general terms here the thorny problem of how the Bible relates our human creaturely capacities to develop creation to the necessary turnabout of becoming saved (salvation), or how the Bible ties in our native ability to grow and test out things with the fundamental process of becoming holy (sanctification). But with the biblical cosmological awareness of human development and historical redemption as a backdrop, let us just look specifically at what the letters Paul brought to book and what Psalm 149 tell us to do about becoming adopted kids of God who will live that way.

Since becoming saved is a gift of God appropriated by a human's simple trust that what the LORD says is certain, becoming saved is not complicated. A person becomes secure in God's everlasting love on the basis of Jesus Christ's death and resurrection. Since becoming holy is an ongoing act of the Holy Spirit's weaning us from our basic attachment to Sin, becoming filled with the fullness of God is time-consuming and difficult.

We resist the leading of God's Word and Spirit from sheer pig-headedness, and saved people often confuse their human responsibility to be single-minded with God's act of salvation (Philippians 1:9-11, 2:12-13), as if we need to win adoption ourselves on a system of credit points. Don't revert to the ABC's of pagan religion, says Paul, to the bondage of do-it-yourself salvation: you have become adopted children of God — remember your baptism (Galatians 3:23-4:11)! Once adopted by God, your sinful acts grieve the Holy Spirit but do not alter the Lord's protective closeness to you and God's having promised you faithful ones an inheritance of victorious glory with Christ. So relax in the freedom Christ won for you — walk around in the spirit of grateful love (Galatians 5:1-6, 13-18).

"Adoption" gives a warm colour to what it means that God is "covenantal." A person becomes related to God. Abraham and David are woodpile relation, but Christ is our brother! "Adoption" also gives prayer its proper, unpressured setting.

To pray is to talk to our heavenly Father, to plead for things, as kids do, and say "thank you," to ask the hard, unanswerable questions. Or, as Psalm 131 puts it, "Like a child quieted at its mother's breast, so now, after my pompous, hard-nosed kick, I am quieted down, close to you, LORD." To pray is to utter Psalm 39, Psalm 51 and Psalms 91, 68, 139, 148 and 149 without fear but with a groaning confidence because, after all, we belong to God's family! Being adopted by God spells freedom from your needing to guarantee your acceptance by God!

That's why God's children breathe a spirit of joy and generosity, of singing and dancing, celebrating the Lord's goodness, including at night on their beds, it says (Psalm 149:5)! Our groaning at our incomplete redemption is also swallowed up in the sureness and laughter of the victory against evil cultural powers, which judgement the LORD will have us administer (see 1 Corinthians 6:1-3, Revelation 21:22-27). Even our human suffering and disappointments will be turned by Christ's incredible plenitude into thanksgiving, says Scripture (Psalm 56:8-11, Philippians 1:27-30, 1 Peter 4:12-19).

So the point for us who want our daily professional activity to be of a piece with our actual adoption by God is for that professional activity to show a human face, a face that is becoming redeemed rather than defaced. And that holds true no matter what one does.

Philosophical activity — my own profession — that shows it is being freed from the traditions of men and is becoming a witness to the LORD's glory will not be uptight about its conceptual impasses and its ongoing, sometimes improvised analytic solutions because the dated, faulty philosophy of God's children will still give good direction and exude a spirit of genuine analytic praise and wisdom.

Christian (that is, scripturally led) buying and selling will be without guile. Commerce, real estate, merchandising carried on by God's family of adopted business people and customers will not be selfish, aggressive, reproachful and smug in critique of the secularist's hardsell, but it will be generous, kind and cheerful. The "yellow pages" and small print of a redemptive communion will not boast prooftexts and a closed club of kosher saints who "take good care of one another," but it will be especially serviceable to those who are outside the faith so that God's children may exercise thrift and export (give away!) the biblical full-measure.

Journalists, bankers, nurses, students — anyone with employment who lives by Ephesians 2, Romans 8 and Psalm 149 — will relax and be able to be patient, compassionate and sure because they can rejoice that their reporting and financing, medical help, studies and whatever they do is not their own, but belongs to our faithful Saviour Jesus Christ.

Dear LORD,
Please fold us in your arms,
and walk along with us carried on your shoulders
so that we can feel how close to you we really are.
And take us by the hand and teach us to do what we do
so it makes you smile.
And protect us, LORD, *from pretending to others*
we have to be strong, grown up and mature to be a Christian
believer.
Save us from trying to save ourselves.
Fill us with the relief adopted kids know,
that you truly wanted us as your children,
and we are yours for keeps.
We ask these things, LORD,
so we may come to rest in your all-powerful arms of love.
Amen.

PSALM 131

1 LORD, my heart is hum - bled now: I have
2 Like a child near moth - er's breast I have

stopped my haugh - ty frown, curbed my dreams to
found con - tent - ment, rest. All God's folk, hope

fit my gifts; yes, at last I have calmed down.
in the LORD; soon God's rule will be re - stored.

Text: Psalm 131; vers. Calvin Seerveld, 1982, ©
Tune: attr. Martin Herbst, 1676

77 77 AUS DER TIEFE

5. NEIGHBOUR-HOODED

Holly Risch, *Man eating at table* (1981) Drawing, gouache, mixed media, in the home of Inès and Calvin Seerveld-Naudin ten Cate, Toronto

The man determinedly set to eat his plate of fish is not alone. Behind his arm with the knife, to the side, is an apparition of a human in need, hands clasped, patient and resigned. On the other side an out-stretched hand entreats for food. The painting on the blood-red back wall shows humans with only one leg over a high obstacle. Holly Risch is asking whether we who eat meals are not convicts at our dinner tables, criminally heedless and isolated from our woebegone neighbours at large in God's broken world.

NEIGHBOURHOODED

A nother feature peculiar to humanity on which the Bible gives directing light is our being neighbourhooded on earth. It is so that animals run in packs, fly in swarms or are tended in flocks. Plants are rooted in the ground with others of their species and genera. How minerals are associated depends upon their geological strata; minerals are grouped together only by virtue of their lustre, cleavage, hardness and colour. But humans have a specially bonded, poignantly intimate connection: humans are inescapably neighbourhooded.

Let us hear the gospel according to Luke, and then a paragraph from Isaiah.

The context Luke gives to the story Jesus told about the tender-hearted Samaritan is very important for us to notice so that we will hear the specific Word on neighbouring the Scripture gives rather than take the passage as a detached humanist manifesto for global, humanitarian relief. For our purposes — so we hear God speaking to us — it would be very exact if our marginal gloss titled this section of Luke 10 "A story of the tender-hearted, despised businessman, as told by Jesus to the Christian lawyer or academic."

We read from Luke 10, starting at verse 25. This is the Word of God:

At that point a certain learned fellow of the lawyer type stood up to put Jesus through the wringer. "Rabbi," he said, "what do I have to have done if I am to inherit eternal life?"

Jesus said to the learned fellow of the lawyer type, "What is written in the law? How do you interpret its reading?"

And the learned fellow of the lawyer type answered,

"Love the LORD your God passionately with your whole heart, with your whole soul, with the whole of your strength — that includes with your whole understanding consciousness — and love your neighbour as intensely as you love yourself."

Jesus said to the learned fellow of the lawyer type, "You have given the orthodox answer. Do that and you will live."

Now this learned fellow of the lawyer type wanted to show he knew what he was talking about, so he said to Jesus, "But who out there is my neighbour?"

[It was a controversy of the day whether Gentiles were "neighbours" to believing Jews, whether convicted criminals, heretics, habitual sinners were "neighbours" — what are the limits to "neighbours" out there?]

Catching the drift of his remark, Jesus answered with a story.

"Once upon a time a certain man went from Jerusalem down to Jericho, and he walked into a group of bandits who, after stripping him of his clothes and beating him badly, went away, leaving him behind half-dead.

"By coincidence a certain priest was travelling down that road. When the priest saw the half-dead man, he walked past after crossing over to the opposite side of the road. In the same way a Levite who came to the place and saw the half-dead fellow also passed by after crossing over to the opposite side of the road.

"A certain Samaritan (businessman) journeying along came to the same spot. Upon seeing the naked, beaten fellow, he was moved to a tender compassion. The Samaritan, going to the beaten fellow, put underclothes around, binding up the fellow's wounds (Greek: traumata), pouring on healing oil and disinfecting wine. Then the Samaritan, setting the fellow on his own personal mule, brought him to an inn — he took good care of the poor fellow.

"On the next day the Samaritan, coming up with enough money for a fortnight, gave it to the innkeeper and said, 'Take good care of this fellow, and whatever more you have to spend, I will reimburse you when I come again.'"

(Jesus asked) "Which of these three seems to you to have become a neighbour for the one who fell into the group of bandits?"

And the learned fellow of the lawyer type said, "The one who showed mercy to the unfortunate derelict."

Jesus said to the learned fellow of the lawyer type, "Move on now, and you do things the same way."

Now as Jesus and his disciples went on their way Jesus came into a certain village where a woman by the name of Martha received him hospitably in her house. Martha also had a sister called Mary who went to sit down near the feet of the Lord to hear what Jesus would say.

Now Martha became upset, being overbusy with so much serving (of all the people). Abruptly stopping by Jesus she said, "My LORD, doesn't it bother you that my sister has deserted me so that I serve the people all alone? Tell her then to lend a hand along with me!"

The Lord replied to her, "Martha, Martha, you are over-anxious and disturbed about so many, many things. Just a few things, or only one matter really, is needed. Mary has chosen the good part, which shall not be taken away from her."

Luke 10:25-42

Now comes the passage Jesus used in part as text for a sermon he gave in his hometown of Nazareth (see Luke 4:14-30). This too is the Word of God for us to hear and appropriate:

The Spirit of the LORD God, my Lord, is upon me
because the LORD God has personally anointed me
to bring good news to those who are meekly humbled.
The LORD has commissioned me to bind up and dress with cloths
the heart of those who have been shattered.
(The LORD has sent me out) to proclaim aloud
to those who have been taken captive, "You are free!"
and to those who are tied up in knots, "You are loosened, unbound!"
(The LORD has consecrated me) to proclaim
"A year of Jubilee from the LORD!"
yes, "A Day of punishing judgement from our God!"

so that all those who have been grieving shall be comforted.
(The L ORD slowly poured oil over all my body so that I might)
bring about for those who are grieving and have been hurt for
the sake of Zion:
replace the dirty ashes on their heads with a tiara,
turn their weeping chagrin into a sweet-smelling oil of
celebration,
exchange the depressed spirit (which enfolds them) for a
cloak of laughing hallelujahs!
so that people will call out to these who were in mourning,
"You are solid oak trees of what is tried-and-true,"
a veritable planting of the L ORD simply to display God's glory!

Isaiah 61:1-3

Neighbourhoodedness (Mitsein) is given with human nature.
Because every man and woman is personally answerable to the
double-barrelled command of the L ORD God — love me totally,
first and above all, and love and respect your fellow human as
intently as you love and respect yourself (see Deuteronomy 6:4-
9 and Leviticus 19:15-18) — that central command of God
makes all humans inescapably neighbours.

Especially academic types, and their wives or husbands,
who are accustomed to making fine distinctions and have an
educated sense of reserve and privacy, seem to have trouble
with the apparent indiscriminate giving away of love that Jesus
stands for. On top of that, we who are traditional orthodox
believers tend to want to have things clear so we know where
we stand. "What do I have to have done if I am to inherit eternal
life?" We don't want to leave anything undone. At the same
time, we don't want to be crazy zealots, either. Exactly how are
we to understand some of the extreme statements of the Christ:
if your eye becomes lustful, cut it out and throw it away lest you
go as a whole corporeal person to hell (Matthew 5:27-29); if you
had just a smidgin of genuine faith you could say to the
mountain, "Move over" — nothing will be impossible for you
(Matthew 17:14-20); you only lack one thing — sell everything
you have, distribute the proceeds to the poor; just follow me
(Luke 18:18-27)?

We say: "Must be a metaphor or some kind of idiomatic expression of the day we haven't as yet figured out from the Dead Sea Scrolls how to read...."

God's Word of Luke 10 is filling out what it means to be a disciple following the LORD Jesus Christ. A cornerstone of the Christ's message and ministry is the marriage of Deuteronomy 6:4-9 with Leviticus 19:15-18, so that those who have ears to hear let their whole-hearted, whole-bodied love for the LORD infuse their being engaged with fellow humans. Simultaneously, those faithful ones do not let their self-respect and outgoing compassion for the neighbour become either a depressing obligation or a means of their salvation, because living out our neighbourhoodedness is really only bodying forth our utter gratitude to the LORD for having become one of God's adopted children.

One of the happiest things that Luke tells us about this double-single Rule of the Lord Jesus Christ in the world is that for the kids of the kingdom who administer its regime of merciful judgement and hearty joy, there are no limits! You will be and may be completely unconstrained in exercising the fruits of the Holy Spirit (see Paul's joke in Galatians 5:22-23) — that's what being a neighbour means!

The learned fellow of the lawyer type set up roadblocks in his discriminating mind. He was giving Jesus a litmus test of the rabbi's orthodoxy — how straight or equivocal are you on the question of "neighbourhood," sir? Do you include prostitutes out there? Prodigal sons and prodigal daughters — are you soft on morality? Do "neighbours" include the hated Samaritans who years ago collaborated with the Babylonian troops who occupied the Holy Land?

Jesus punctured the learned fellow's show of pride and knowledgeable orthodoxy by getting religiously behind the academic mask, piercing to the heart of this learned fellow's fence-building mentality: you need to activate *yourself* as neighbour! In fact, it's possible you may have to realize that if and when you are waylaid and done in, you may need to be open to the help of those whom you judge, hate and despise. "Neighbour" is not a class of approved people. Neighbourhooding is a glorious gift to human nature: the opening to give to and receive from one's fellow human what is needed.

But don't pride yourself on supplying needs (see Matthew 6:1-4), Luke's narrative continues.   Don't ever think your diaconal activism, maybe yours alone, is instituting the kingdom of our LORD and God in history.   Never pit neighbouring against hearing continually afresh the living Word of God — this is the truth with which Luke uses the Martha-Mary incident to round out Christ's wise reply to the bad question of "What must I have gotten done to inherit eternal life?" Luke is not giving priority to the contemplative life (Mary's quiet listening) next to the practical life (Martha's waiting tables). The whole thrust and context of Luke's extended, God-breathed account anchors neighbouring in prayer and praising the LORD (see Luke 11:1-13) and exposits discipleship as the gift of fulfilling our neighbourhooded humanity, secured by God's adoption (see Luke 10:17-20).

God's acts bring in the Rule of Jesus Christ on earth. Our efforts do not do it. So there should be neither calculation nor mania in our being a neighbour. Instead, if we hear and obey the good news from Luke and Isaiah, then our neighbouring takes on the spendthrift freedom and heedless exuberance of giving away a respecting love to those humans who are least able or are unwilling to respond as neighbours — the robbed and beaten destitute of the earth, and our enemies. To be a neighbour to those who are hateful or half-dead drives academicians of the lawyer type and Martha busybodies up the wall. But such neighbouring is the very life of God's adopted children, because neighbouring the handicapped and terribly helpless and those who persecute God's faithful ones confirms, ratifies, our bond of intimate love with the LORD (see Luke 14:12-14, Matthew 5:43-48), who in Jesus Christ is the Lord of all humans and would that neighbours become brothers and sisters.

Any seasoned teacher knows that teaching means you wash the feet of your students. In line with the texts before us you could also understand and describe teaching, or Christian leadership of any sort, as a kind of neighbouring, where you bind up the wounds, the traumata, of the younger generation who come to you, having been damaged at home or in earlier

Rembrandt van Rijn, *Christus predikend* [La Petite Tombe] (c. 1652) Etching, National Gallery of Art, gift of W.G. Russell Allen, Washington, D.C.

Rembrandt situates Christ in the press of ordinary people. Women close by are absorbed with his message of forgiveness. One elderly gentleman stands up startled, and leans forward to participate in the blessing. The sceptical bystanders are on the other side, finger and hands to chin, cavalier. But other people are not hell to Rembrandt: unbelievers and even enemies are neighbours when they cross your path.

schools. Blessed are those who neighbour the poor people who have lost their way and become captives or have been damaged in the arts, or in the marketplace, or in the minefield of politics. And it is a wonderful occupation to be anointed by the Spirit of the LORD to bring healing and comfort to those with need, to give good direction and to announce the coming jubilee and judgement for music, commerce, family relations, philosophy — you name it.

The final Word right now on our human, neighbourhooded nature, however, is truly bittersweet. Acting as tenderhearted neighbour in our day and age may bring you grief. If you lovingly and caringly expose how his or her idol has mesmerized your fellow human into becoming like it, the militarist may shoot to kill, the rationalist may deny you a podium at which to think and the charlatan may mock you to pieces. If you stop in the bad section of the road between Jerusalem and Jericho to assist some lonely traveller who has been brutalized, while you are absorbed in offering first aid, the institutional terrorists may return and get you, too. Many of your brothers and sisters may pooh-pooh this wide-open neighbourhood ministry as non-essential and run you out of town (as the believers of Nazareth did to Jesus when he spoke on Isaiah 61 and implied that none of their sick were healed because they didn't have the humbled faith to receive such neighbouring! See Luke 4:24-30 and Luke 10:1-16). To show compassion today, to forgive a sinner seventy times seven times, that is, "forever," is to become exploited yourself.

But such suffering, borne for the sake of showing Jesus Christ's holy, redeeming Rule of love, is a mark of humanity rich with scriptural promises of great blessing (Romans 8:15-18, Philippians 1:27-30, James 1:2-4, 1 Peter 4:12-16). In fact, for any person who as an adopted child of God in neighbourhooding to others' needs has been stripped of privilege, has been battered back and forth by the competitive professional worlds we inhabit, who has been and is now left lonely, somewhat humiliated, bypassed by the good people on the way to the temple: the Spirit of the LORD God is upon me to promise you relief and protection with our Lord within the genuine body of Jesus Christ. The ashes of mourning on your head are becoming diamonds of a crown, and the depressed spirit that sometimes stifles your joy will be turning into a cloak of laughing hallelujahs.

Blessed are the faithful neighbours, for they shall experience shalom and the communion of saints (see Matthew 5:3-16, Romans 13:8-10). You are solid oak trees of what is tried and true, a veritable planting of the LORD, given a history as a human simply to display God's glory.

Dear LORD God,
Sometimes we would just like to be alone,
free from the press of all the other people all around,
pushing and shoving their needs and wants in our face.
But we pray, dear God,
that your Holy Spirit will give us the strength and the wisdom
to love our neighbours,
especially the ones that get in our way every day.
Give us the grace to exercise our neighbourhoodedness
in neighbouring acts,
so that the love of Christ will give us who are inescapably together
a fellowship that celebrates you as our common LORD.
Make us solid oak trees, please, who give good shade
because our roots grow deep in your word of truth.
We pray in Jesus' name.
Amen.

Edward Hagedorn, *New Growth* (1970) Construction, acrylic painting, pipe, mixed media [now lost]

Living plants make good neighbours, because they regenerate the air we humans and animals breathe. Artist Hagedorn celebrates God's grace that allows shoots of grass and tendrils of green to sprout in the filthy muck of industrial wastes. Meanwhile, tanks of chemicals appear mistily through the blue like ghostly missiles on target for pollution. New growth enters the neighbourhood of earth we humans are poisoning.

SONG OF ROMANS 8

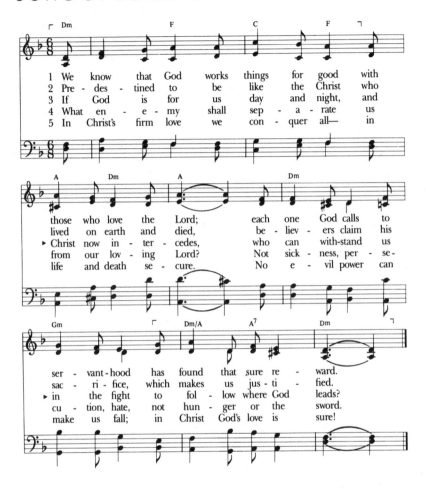

1 We know that God works things for good with
2 Pre - des - tined to be like the Christ who
3 If God is for us day and night, and
4 What en - e - my shall sep - a - rate us
5 In Christ's firm love we con - quer all— in

those who love the Lord; each one God calls to
lived on earth and died, be - liev - ers claim his
► Christ now in - ter - cedes, who can with-stand us
from our lov - ing Lord? Not sick - ness, per - se -
life and death se - cure. No e - vil power can

ser - vant-hood has found that sure re - ward.
sac - ri - fice, which makes us jus - ti - fied.
► in the fight to fol - low where God leads?
cu - tion, hate, not hun - ger or the sword.
make us fall; in Christ God's love is sure!

Text: Roman 8:28-39; vers. Calvin Seerveld, 1985
Tune: Calvin Seerveld, 1985; harm. Dale Grotenhuis, 1986
Text and music © 1986, Calvin Seerveld

CM LESTER

6. IN THE ORDER OF MELCHIZEDEK

Georges Rouault, *Il serait si doux d'aimer* (1914-48) Aquatint, Rosenwald Collection, National Gallery of Art, Washington, D.C.

Loving is being close and accessible, protective and giving, but not constraining. The arm of the mother in Rouault's ensemble gestures away from the child nestling at her breast, toward the outer world fraught with miseries, like war. "It would be so sweet to love," says this bittersweet art reluctantly. Parents truly love their children when they lay down their life for their offspring, that is, firmly sacrifice attachment in order to outfit the younger ones with a wisdom that will endure, as wary as a snake and as without guile as a dove.

IN THE ORDER OF
MELCHIZEDEK

W̲e shall read perhaps the most important psalm in the book of the Psalms, number 110, and then a few well-known passages from the Newer Testament canon found in letters of Peter and Paul. Can we hear without distortion the prime calling of humanity as Scripture discloses it?

Imagine the psalmist to be reporting first to King David what the LORD God has specially revealed. Then imagine the psalmist addressing God's people about the LORD God's anointed leader.

This is what the LORD God says to my Lord:
"Sit at my right hand until I have put down your enemies as a footstool for your feet."
The LORD will give free reign to the official sceptre of your power, (David).
Go ahead, rule from Zion in the thick of your enemies!
On D-Day your folk will be willingness itself,
wrapped in the splendours of consecration.
Just as dew (springs) from the womb of a sunrise,
so shall your youthful strength surprise you.
(I repeat,) this is what the LORD has sworn, and God will not have second thoughts (about it):
"Henceforth you are a priest forever in the order of Melchizedek."

[to the people]

My Lord is at your right hand!
My Lord shall break kings to pieces in the day of his anger.
My Lord shall set things straight in the nations filled with corpses!

My Lord shall shatter (those who are) head over most of the
earth —
(God's anointed one) shall be able to drink water from the
running stream nearby the way (of judgement):
that is why God's anointed one shall be able to hold the head
up high!

Psalm 110

You are a chosen kind of humanity, a royal priesthood, a holy
peoplehood, a folk intended to be God's peculiar family, so
that you might broadcast the powerful glories of the One
who called you out of darkness into God's wonderful light.
Once upon a time you were not a people, but now you are
the people of God. Once you were not recipients of mercy,
but now you have actually received mercy.

1 Peter 2:9-10

This is the picture: if anyone is in Christ, he or she is a new
creation. What's old has gone: new things have come! All
this change is from God, who reconciled us to very God once
upon a time through Christ and gave us the ministry of
reconciliation. That is, God was busy in Christ reconciling
the world to God: God was not busy counting up the failings
and lapses in faith of all the people.

God has entrusted us with the Word of reconciliation.
That means that we serve as ambassadors of Christ: God
exhorts, pleads, comforts through us. (So) we urge you, for
Christ's sake! let yourselves be reconciled to God. God took
the one who experientially never knew sin, God took him as
guilty sinner instead of us so that we in Christ might become
representative of God's way of making things right.

...Although we walk around in the flesh, we do not make
war in flesh-and-blood fashion. The weapons of our warfare
are not the carnal ones, but are God-all-powerful ones for
demolishing whatever people take to make their strongholds.
With our God-all-powerful weapons we are engaged in
breaking down reasoned arguments and every sophisticated,

stuck-up pretension which blocks and defies authentic, first-hand knowledge of God; we are struggling to bring every human conception, to take every intended human project away captive to make it obedient to Christ.

2 Corinthians 5:17-21, 10:3-5

According to the first chapter of the Acts of the Apostles, Jesus spent the important forty days left on earth between his resurrection from the dead and ascension to God's right hand speaking to his disciples particularly about the crucial matters of the kingdom Rule of God (Acts 1:3). And it is not for nothing that the first verse of Psalm 110 is the most-quoted Old Testament line in the New Testament: "Sit at my right hand (says the LORD) until I have put down your enemies as a footstool for your feet." The revelation that the Rule of God's Anointed One, the Messiah in David's line, the resurrected Lord Jesus Christ, is sure was a revelation that gave great comfort to the early church.

But the Jewish Zealots also loved that Old Testament line: Wait for God to knock off the Romans, and we'll use them for footstools! Such a reading of God's kingdom Rule on earth, like a humanist recitation of Psalm 8 that would melt the LORD God's name down into the lordly power of us enlightened humans who dictate terms to animals, plants and planets misrepresents the scriptural truth. The Jews who rejected Christ's gospel overlooked verse 4 of Psalm 110, with the injunction to be a *priestly* king. That's precisely why the New Testament letter to "the Hebrews" makes so much of Melchizedek, who was a priest-king (Hebrews 4:14-8:13, Genesis 14:17-24). The kingdom Rule of the LORD God revealed in Jesus Christ is not that of a warlord, an overlord, a strongman, a king or queen who rules by fleshly force. The kingdom of the true God is a Rule that sets things right in which the earthly vice-regents, those who are anointed as priests — Paul's image is "ambassadors" — mediate the bestowal of God's blessings to other humans in God's world who are ungrateful misfits or who often bring the LORD blemished sacrifices.

The order of Melchizedek is God's appointed commission

for human leadership in history. We humans do not rule creation by divine right. And the rule on the earth delegated by the LORD to humanity since the fall of Eve and Adam is not one of domination, but one of reconciliation. Just as Christ did not belong to the priesthood which the sons of Aaron inherited by right of blood, but was instead a priest-king like Melchizedek, begotten mysteriously — as it were directly by God — who sacrificed himself and put the regular priests of inherited privilege out of business, just so, it is revealed, the position of leadership which goes with human nature fulfilled in Christ is most fundamentally a Rule characterized by mercy, not mastery. Humans called to rule by the LORD have no claim in themselves, no absolute title, to be rulers. If humans pretend to be kings or priests on their own, they will endlessly try, like Aaron's unregenerated seed, to patch things up and make things good, get them to run well, but there will be no rest, no blessing of the kind that comes with being a humbled leader. Only when the prime calling of humanity to rule in God's world is exercised by following the lead of Christ's Melchizedekian royal priesthood, where the human ruler becomes himself or herself a *living* sacrifice (Romans 12:1-2) and ruling is conceived and practised as an intercessory ministry — only then is the basic office of humanity rightly assumed.

There is no question in Scripture that the call for humans to rule creation takes power, the kind of power that cuts down trees into planks, milks animals, constructs dikes against floods, is able to fashion stories to enthrall listeners, a power that comes to project the human voice through the air to the other side of a continent, transport people on wheels, make plans against famine, stop aggression. To rule among creatures takes a measure of control, and control assumes an appropriate strength. Because evil still is at large in the world before Christ returns with an army of angels to finish it off, the God-awful power and strength humans can command often turns exploitive rather than being a consecrated channel for conveying peace. Whether "my Lord" in Psalm 110 is referring (see Psalm 2) to the sinful, anointed King David, or the scapegoat-Melchizedek Jesus Christ, or to the born-again creation called "Christian" (see Acts 11:19-26), the power which God's

Rembrandt van Rijn, *Christus de zieken genezende* [The hundred guilder print] (1659) Etching, The Rosenwald Collection, National Gallery of Art, Washington, D.C.

Rembrandt etches the commanding mercy of Jesus Christ with a sure modesty. There is no baroque grandeur in this world of unfortunates: the sick, the handicapped, the impoverished, the lonely and rejected, stream in from the darkness beseeching Christ who gives away light to the world. Dog and child, beggar and rich young ruler, learned scribes and corpulent fool: all attend Christ's unpretentious, unobtrusive ministry. To heal wounds and forgive sin, to teach humility and instill hope, as Christ did on earth, is to rule by serving—Melchizedek.

anointed ones employ, says the psalm, is always mindful of the Lord's timing to conclude things, and is to be aware that human leaders in Christ's body are to reach out with the power that sets things right by showing mercy. That's why the adulterous murderer and psalmist David, like the sinless Messiah Jesus, the denying apostle Peter, the former persecutor Paul, Mary Magdalene and whoever, though sinful, comes to walk in God's wonderful light, shall be able to hold the head up high when the final judgement comes: they lived and had their meaning under the order of Melchizedek.

So what concretely does Scripture ask of us today if the people of God are to be essentially Melchizedekian priests? Granted that the people of God in history are a select humanity — the fallen humanity which in spite of its fragility, because of its new adoption by the LORD in Jesus Christ, is anointed to work out its hallelujahs, neighbouring to one another and caring for things as a priestly programme of reconciliation. What concretely does the Word of reconciliation and mercy mean for us?

It means first for those of us humans who confess Jesus Christ as Lord and practise the historical Reformation version of the biblical faith, that we need to be in a living communion with God while we think and argue, work, eat and drink, joke, live or die. There needs to be a vibrant glory, a quiet lustre of outgoing love deeply motivating and suffusing our deeds, an unspoken testimony that our life is indeed lived with God for Christ's sake alone and is not a partial attempt to establish ourselves.

I'm not talking up a sanctimonious halo of kindly intentions. The Word of reconciliation and mercy does not call us to have a sweet attitude or an irenic disposition. Mercy in the Scriptures is an enabling deed, fermenting a bond of trust. Mercy is actually giving undeserved favour that brings someone else on course. To show mercy is to atone for someone else yourself, to cover and make good for the sins of another. The Word of reconciliation we humans are to broadcast, because we have ourselves actually received mercy from the LORD, is to carry on and follow through on Christ's making good for sinners.

The disciples on the road to Emmaeus told Jesus that their Psalm 110:1 millennial expectations for Israel to put down the Romans had fizzled, but Jesus tried to teach them verse 4, that God's people had really triumphed in his death and resurrection because now they could overthrow the Romans! They could do this by preaching and showing even to Romans the gospel deed of repentance and forgiveness, that is, mercy (Luke 24:21, 44-48).

Christ wants mercy from us on earth, not bits and pieces of a glass-cathedral sacrifice, say, of a Christian philosophy, over-insured by scholastic taboos (see Hosea 6:4-6, Matthew 9:10-13, 12:1-8). If our philosophical reflection on being human in Christian perspective is an act of mercy, however, that is, if our anthropological theory starts to give conceptual hope and healing direction to those thinking about humanity who are lost in the trackless labyrinth of God-forsaken traditions, then we will have been faithful ambassadors of Jesus Christ. If our redemptive theoretical thinking gives glimmers of conceptual hope by exorcising current anthropological theories and by pointing erring thinkers to a grasp of being human that helps them know forgiveness and see the necessity of a reconciled humanity, then we will have been "ruling philosophers," who have served God and neighbour by doing analytic deeds that prove charitably true because we will have been vessels of mercy.

Sinful humans — whether political manipulators, immoral journalists, secularistic thinkers or whatever — are not the antagonists of God's people. Those who receive God's mercy contend with the ideological principalities and subtle evil powers that tyrannize the consciousness and acts of sinful humans, including the saints (Ephesians 6:12). As we earnestly fight against the strongholds that oppress men and women, that suppress humans from living a redeemed human life, we must remember two things: first, whatever human deeds we take captive in Christ's name we take captive not to kill but to make alive; and second, the God-all-powerful weapons we use to expose the vainglory of the godless and ourselves are precisely the Spirit-filled Word-directives of God (Ephesians 6:10-20), not the weapons of unholy force and deceit.

So Melchizedek-priestly humans are called by our Scripture not to fight fire with fire, terrorism with terrorism, rationalism with more perfect rationalism, split-second communications that superficialize with still quicker, lightning-like communication. The royal priesthood is directed to fight fire with the water of forgiveness lest we have only a scorched earth left. The believer awarded the Order of Melchizedek is asked to fight arguments not with better arguments but with insight, since being bested at argument never induced a human to love the truth. Christ's ambassadors will fight the secularized pragmatic quantification of knowledge and speech not by being "tops in the field" but by redirecting knowledge-gathering and by selecting differently the news for distribution within a labour-intensive, face-to-face teaching and telling that keep knowledge and information open to a homely wisdom.

All our up-to-date reforming rule of culture will still be vain, unless it honours the Name of our LORD by being a reconciling act of mercy.

O LORD!
Thank you that we do not have to play boss in the world.
Thank you that your Rule is one of mercy,
and that your justice we may learn to institute on the earth
is a justice meant to bring life.
Thank you, LORD, that we can be new creatures,
humans who have been graciously, unmeritedly adopted by the Christ
in order to give away the good news of reconciliation with God.
Help us to fight not people but the evil powers that captivate people,
including ourselves.
Give us a double portion, Lord, of your Spirit,
for the hard times ahead,
so we may see clearly that your victorious Rule is sure,
and we may drink deeply of the water that shall keep us from ever being thirsty again.
We thank you in the name of Jesus Christ.
Amen.

PSALM 110

1. "Sit at my right hand," said the LORD to my Lord,
2. Your youth - ful strength shall come like dew at sun - rise
3. The sov - ereign Lord stands guard for your pro - tec - tion;
4. The LORD makes cov - e - nant with God's a - noint - ed

"While I sub - ject your foes be - neath your feet."
to lead your pledged folk read - y for the fight.
he shall wreak ven - geance on the judge - ment Day.
who fol - low Christ, the true Mel - chiz - e - dek:

The LORD shall bless your rul - ing from Mount Zi - on
The LORD has sworn, God nev - er shall re - voke it:
The Lord shall smash all mil - i - tar - y for - ces
daunt - ed in strug - gle, you shall drink fresh wa - ter,

— right in the thick of en - e - my de - ceit.
"You are a priest — king called to acts of right."
which proud - ly feast — kill, waste the meek as prey.
and hold your heads high, safe as God's e - lect.

Text: Psalm 110; vers. Calvin Seerveld 1980 ©
Tune: Louis Bourgeois, 1551; harm. Dale Grotenhuis, 1988

11 10 11 10 GENEVAN 110

Gerald Folkerts, *A Double Portion* (1986) Pencil and charcoal drawing, in home of Inès and Calvin Seerveld -Naudin ten Cate, Toronto

When Elisha received the mantle of fiery Elijah's ministry, Elisha was tempted to go double or nothing with miracles. But the worlds without end need to have their vessels for oil and water filled, even if it be by the ravens from heaven. Elisha came to learn too that God speaks not so much in the whirlwind and the fire as in the life-giving voice of shalom: good food for the hungry, birth for the barren, healing for the leper who is an enemy. Folkerts gives cosmic scope to the prophetic, redemptive work of reconciliation in God's world.

A HYMN OF PASSION

1. When Eve with A - dam dis - o - beyed, they spoiled cre - a - tion God had made. The gra - cious LORD so loved the world God sent the Son to be be - trayed, who gave his life for debts un - paid.

2. Like root from dry ground God's Son grew in - to a suf - fering, serv - ing Jew. He fed the poor folk, healed the sick, for - gave the out - cast, made lives new, and taught dis - ci - ples what was true.

3. On aw - ful Fri - day we call good the Ro - mans hung the Christ on wood. Re - spect - ed peo - ple mocked at God, but Je - sus sad - ly un - der - stood his death did what no sin - ner could.

4. As we re - call the Sa - viour's pain, whose life and death God did or - dain, re - mem - ber that the LORD a - rose, and all our work is not in vain if we in faith ac - cept his reign.

5. So bro - thers, sis - ters, dry your tears; help neigh - bours put a - way their fears. Come serve the res - ur - rect - ed LORD, and live as sured as judge - ment nears when Christ tri - um - phant re - ap - pears.

Text: Calvin Seerveld, 1984, ©
Tune: attr. Matthäus Greiter, Strassburger Gesangbüchern, 1552; harm. Dale Grotenhuis

8 8 8 8 8 IN DICH HABE ICH GEHOFFET

7.PREGNANT

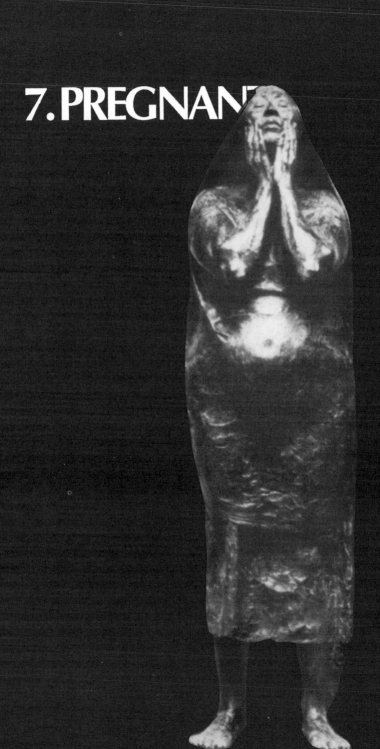

Francisco Zuñiga, *Standing Woman* (1976) Bronze, New York, Sindin Galleries

The church of Jesus Christ is like a woman with child whose bridegroom has not yet shown up. Zuñiga's woman of bronze has an ancient feel of being shamefully hard worn but strong, roughly used but royal in bearing. From the arms and hands that caress her uplifted face to the bare feet planted surely on the ground her whole maternal body gives evidence of a focused readiness for what will eventually come. The glory of bearing fruit on time, however, entails the hard labour of an advent.

PREGNANT

L et us read three fragments surrounding what I find to be a sevenfold refrain in the book of Ecclesiastes, which constitutes the key to the book's deeply comforting message in the hardest of times.

The opening verses of Chapter 3 are the famed litany of what seems to be a time for good and a time for bad in the world, a time of accomplishment offset by a time of failure. This is the Word of God that follows:

What's the use! What's left over from the labouring to which a man and a woman exert themselves?

I have come to understand this miserable problem which God has given to the sons and daughters of humanity to bother them with:
Everything God has ever done is very good — beautiful, done at its right time.
On top of that, God has opened the human heart to this God-timing (eternity)
— I don't mean that the human can find out exactly what God has actually been doing from beginning to end —

I have come to know experientially that we humans can do nothing good by ourselves, that for a man or a woman even to be glad, to be well-off in life, for anybody even to be able to eat and drink and enjoy good in the press and trouble-some change of daily life: all this is purely a gift of God.
I have come to understand experientially that whatever God does lasts forever
— nothing can be added to it and nothing can be taken away

from it —
God has set things up this way so that men and women will
stand in awe of God.

Whatever is already has been, and whatever is to be already
has become:
God picks up the broken pieces.

...Stand amazed at the great doings of God!
Who indeed could make straight what God has bent! —
On good days be cheerful, and on bad days hang firmly on to
this:
God is the One who makes evil days as well as good days
— this is why humans cannot piece out for themselves
anything of what will follow them....
        Oh, sweet is the light!
How good it is for one's eyes to enjoy the sunlight!
So, if a man or woman lives many years (of sunshine), let that
person joy in them all:
just don't let one forget that the dark days, all those which
turn up like an obscuring mist, will also be many.
        Be joyful then, you younger ones, in your youth!
Let that red pulsing blood in you make you feel good that you
are in your prime —
Do what you really deeply feel like doing! Revel in whatever
your eyes light upon —
just know keenly that for all these matters
God will settle with you on the judgement day....

   Ecclesiastes 3:9-15, 7:13-14, 11:7-9

And now we read the vision of the return of Immanuel and how
God finally completes making the creation new, which is
recorded in a paragraph of Revelation 21. This is the Word of
God:

Then I saw a heavens, new, and an earth, new. The earlier
heavens and the earlier earth have passed away; even the sea
was no longer there. And I saw the holy city Jerusalem, new,

coming down out of the heavens from God, made ready like a bride who has been wonderfully dressed for her husband.
And I heard a great voice from the throne saying:

See that! The tabernacle of God is there among the humans! God will tent among them, and the humans will be God's people, yes, God in person will be right there with them.

God will wipe away completely every tear from their eyes. The death shall be no more! Neither shall there ever be any mourning or crying or troublesome pain any more, because the earlier order of things has passed away.

The One who was seated on the throne said, "You see! I am making everything new!"

The One seated on the throne also said, "Write it down, because these words are trustworthy and utterly true."

The One seated on the throne said directly to me:
"It is finally finished.

"I am the Alpha and the Omega, the Beginning and the End —
I shall give to whoever is thirsty a great gift! (a drink) from the spring of the water of Life.

"Whoever conquers shall inherit all these things, and I will be God for him and for her, and he and she shall be for me children.

"But as for the cowardly, the unfaithful, the disgustingly foul people, (premeditative) murderers, those who fornicate, who are bewitched by drugs, as for the idolaters and all those who are false in word: their lot is in the lake of fire and burning sulphur, which is the second death."

Revelation 21:1-8

Scripture says that to be human is to live in joyful expectation of an everlasting fullness of creaturely glory, rubbing shoulders with the LORD God, our almighty redeeming Creator, on an earth with heavens as marvellous as Paradise, or to have a makeshift existence, as pleasant as one can humanly make it oneself, under the threat of termination, which would render everything fairly meaningless (see Deuteronomy 30:11-20).

Because humans are selfhooded, neighbourhooded, fragile creatures who are personally responsible for answering God's command to rule the earth mercifully, being human is to be ontically pregnant, you might say. That is, humans have to give birth, culturally speaking, and either you labour as an adopted child of God and bear the LORD good fruit, or you remain lost and stuck in sin and breed monsters or miscarry what is stillborn (Genesis 6:1-8, Luke 3:7-9, John 15:1-17, Colossians 1:9-14, James 3:13-18).

The Scripture before us speaks especially to the adopted children of God who are in labour, and offers the vision of certainly becoming wholly new as human creatures while promising the gift of full-bodied shalom, which we may taste in our day and age as joy.

The warning of Revelation 21 about the cowardly unfaithful and those who hate, misrepresent and violate their neighbour concerns believers in Jesus Christ, not disbelievers. The warning is so severe because the apostle John already sees the end, and no matter what their pedigree, if the covenanted followers of Christ who are seduced by secularity and drop out or harden their hearts unrepentantly while making believe they are respectable, pious folk — if the final trumpet sounds and catches them reprobate, as lapsed, apostate church, there is no more hope for them (Revelation 18:21-24, Hebrews 5:11-6:8).

For anyone reading this text who is wearing only a mask of faith, this notice of judgement is still grace, because Revelation 21 may soften our hearts and turn us back into a living communion with the LORD.

The comfort of Revelation 21 to the human body of Melchizedek priests in God's world is incredibly strong because John's vivid vision of a final restoration of creation resonates with multiple passages of Scripture: Isaiah 11-12, 40, 43, 60-62; Habakkuk 3; Zechariah 8, 14; Matthew 24-25; and many more. The whole world will be fashioned new. A new Jerusalem — the holy city where God is surrounded by laughter and praise, thanksgiving and a just government, holy trade, edifying conversation, wholesome food, ample resources, sinless human activity — the heaven of God's administration will settle upon the earth in full public view, and the Light of the world will radiate completely worldwide, world without end.

We know that anybody today who is in Christ is already a new creation (2 Corinthians 5:17). Such a one, rooted in Christ's selfless love, is becoming able to give one's self away, give one's life time away to build up the faith and wisdom of one's neighbour (Ephesians 3:14-19). We also know that anyone today who is an adopted child of God in Jesus Christ has discovered that there is a new, united community of faith where Gentile and Jew, red and yellow, black and white races, poor and rich, educated and untrained, female and male have found a union, a sharing communion of peace that simply puts to shame old-fashioned hegemonies and "arbitrated settlements" (Ephesians 2:11-22, Galatians 3:26-29, 6:11-16). But the time is coming when these thirsty beginnings of newness in right-doing will be flooded by God's gloriously tenting among us fully, and there will be no more exploitation, no more brokenness, no more distress — never!

That Revelation 21 vision of complete healing by the Anointed One at God's right hand, the merciful world-conquerer Jesus Christ — who will refine what he finds and make everything new (see John 3:14-21) — brings us to the poignant gospel of joy revealed in God's Word of Ecclesiastes. According to Scripture, joy is a gift God's children know within and during troubles. It is not a disembodied, unhistorical relief that happily distracts one from reality. Joy is anchored in the certainty that the rescue of Revelation 19-21 is acoming, but joy springs up from the gut-level experience that God knows what God is doing now.

The warm strength that comes to persevere in doing what is biblically right though unpopular at a university, as part of a government or in a marketplace, even though you fail — that strength has the joy of knowing you are being protected by the LORD and by God's angels. The solace that takes time to seep into your lonely consciousness after a loved one has been rudely, untimely snatched from life, a solace born slowly and reluctantly, maybe, out of a conviction that God's hard decisions are still decisions by the LORD whom we can trust, that solace is a quiet joy when it comes, a joy that surpasses both remedial therapy and rational explanation. And the excitement when you discover that you've been married thirty years and didn't realize the wear-and-tear but repaired blessing of there being two of you when one falls down (Ecclesiastes 4:9-12), or the spontaneous rush to celebrate with your friends the minor triumph of having finished a time-consuming article or project — such moments become genuine joy when you catch your breath, smile and sense that it was — no kidding — the Holy Spirit who brought it off!

Ecclesiastes depicts political intrigue, cultural mayhem and atrocities as bad as Dachau and Auschwitz. But under it all, sounding through the dirges of dismay at the corruption of humanity on the earth, is the note of bottom-line joy. As a lightning bug shows us its way on a dark night, this refrain from Ecclesiastes tracks God's direction: On good days be cheerful, you adopted children of God, and on difficult days, bad days and nights, remember, the LORD is in charge of what humans suffer and can do (2:24-26, 3:12-13 and 3:22, 5:18-20, 7:14, 8:15, 9:7-10, 11:9). The simple pleasure of tasting a good green salad or a freshly squeezed orange depends upon the LORD God's sustenance of your palate, stomach juices and winding intestines. And God's awful final judgement is not just to even scores but to heal permanently the bruised spots of your life that you can't get over now. So take comfort, says Ecclesiastes, in the basic creaturely satisfactions God provides and in the living assurance that as you labour in a priestly rule, God does pick up all the broken pieces.

Ecclesiastes 3:15 and Revelation 21:5 proclaim the same truth, one from the underside of human faith in the LORD and the other from the vision of history brought to its completion. That truth is that God picks up the pieces, that Jesus Christ makes everything new. So whatever the LORD has done in our lives, is busy doing in our reading a book, in our coming in or going out of a room — whatever God is doing picking up the pieces and making new will last forever.

Love, faith and hope remain, says the Scripture, even after ecstatic tongue-talk, preaching and hard study cease (1 Corinthians 12:27-13:13). In much the same way Scripture says that it is not letter-perfect research or prize-winning success, but doing what is just, spilling over goodness and being joyful

in the Holy Spirit that are the enduring marks of God's kingdom Rule (Romans 14:13-19). Doing justice to another person's
thought takes patient humility as well as love. Overflowing
shalom is not so much like a second helping of dessert as like
turning the other cheek in a journalistic debate (can you imagine!) and going the extra mile on an irregular idea that results
in wisdom. And joy has nothing to do with becoming a dry-
eyed Stoic analyst, but joy has everything to do with the kind of
thinking that, when it is troubled or sad, has its tears dried by
a fellow believer's insightful comment.

Since "God is our strength and place for taking shelter, a
very sound help in deep trouble, we will not fear though the
earth give way" (Psalm 46:1-2) and our daily professional work
goes to pieces. Under the good news of the refrain of Ecclesiastes and the vision of Revelation 21 we humans need only to
see to it that our whole-bodied service, in which the sinful past
and the holy future are both present, be joyful rather than
frivolous, playful rather than tedious, hopeful rather than
afraid, scripturally directed rather than at loose ends. With
Paul I pray

**that your love (of Christ) may spill over more and more in
knowledge, even in every sensation, so that you may be able
to discern what counts (with God), in order that you may
become single-minded and cause no offence until the day
Christ comes, being filled with the fruit of doing-what-is-
right, (a gift) of Jesus Christ for the praise and glory of God.**

Philippians 1:9-11

ECCLESIASTES REFRAIN

1 God's gift it is to eat and drink, to find true joy in
2 In days of glad pros - per - i - ty give thanks that God en -
3 Our dai - ly deeds are in God's hands, their out - come on the

la - bor. No mat - ter what some - one may think, what
folds you. In days of hard ad - ver - si - ty, re -
mor - row. At times God o - ver - rules our plans to

Refrain

God does lasts for - ev - er.
mem - ber, God still holds you. God's prov - i - dence is
teach us trust through sor - row.

good and wise: God holds to - geth - er all our lives.

Text: based on Ecclesiastes 3:13-15; 7:14; vers. Calvin Seerveld 1985, ©
Tune: attr. Bartolomäus Gesius, 1605; adapt and harm. Dale Grotenhuis, 1985.
© 1987, CRC Publications

87 87 88 MACHS MIT MIR

Unknown photographer, *Egyptian woman* (c. 1950s) De Wijsheid, Phoenix Bijbelpocket, Netherlands

The mysterious composure of a face in hard times has an allure. The human reserve of trusting the faithful God to come through provides a quieting, winsome security for those nearby who are unnerved. This portrait of an Egyptian woman complements the sculpture of Barlach's singing man (on the front cover): a godly steadiness in the sorrows of our sin-plagued world and hope in the voice of human song responding to the love of the LORD's mighty acts fully revealed in Jesus Christ point the Way for us humans to image God in the modern world.

AN ADVENT HYMN

1 O Christ! Come back to save your folk.
2 Dear God, let loose the an - gel hosts;
3 O Spir - it, give dumb - found - ing birth!
4 Dear Lord, con - vert our faith to sight.
5 O Christ! re - move our ad - vent fears.

Burst through the clouds with one clean stroke.
send them to stop all war - like boasts.
▸ Car - pet with green a whole new earth.
Shine with the bril - liance end - ing night.
Bol - ster our hope, ex - cite our cheers.

Un - furl the glo - ry prom - ised us.
Star - tle the na - tions filled with hate.
▸ Re - deem the rain - bows in the skies:
Win now the wick - ed chaff from wheat.
Bring on full life both new and free.

Sur - prise with joy those keep - ing trust.
Res - cue the meek while we still wait.
▸ wipe a - way tears from all our eyes.
Har - vest the world; make us com - plete.
Trum - pet at last the ju - bi - lee!

Text: Calvin Seerveld, 1983, ©
Tune: *Gesangbuch*, Augsburg, 1666; harm. Dale Grotenhüis, 1985.
Harmonization © 1987, CRC Publications

LM O HEILAND, REISS DIE HIMMEL AUF

CATALOGUE OF ILLUSTRATIONS

LIST OF PSALMS, HYMNS AND SONGS